Cesar Chavez
Champion for Civil Rights

by Anne Roome and Joanne Mattern

Content Consultant
Nanci R. Vargus, Ed.D.
Professor Emeritus, University of Indianapolis

Reading Consultant
Jeanne M. Clidas, Ph.D.
Reading Specialist

Children's Press®
An Imprint of Scholastic Inc.

Library of Congress Cataloging-in-Publication Data

Roome, Anne Ross, author.
Cesar Chavez/by Anne Roome and Joanne Mattern; poem by Jodie Shepherd.
    pages cm. — (Rookie biographies)
Includes bibliographical references and index.
ISBN 978-0-531-22546-2 (library binding : alk. paper) — ISBN 978-0-531-22635-3 (pbk. : alk. paper)
    1. Chavez, Cesar, 1927-1993—Juvenile literature. 2. Labor leaders—United States—Biography—
Juvenile literature. 3. Mexican American migrant agricultural laborers—Biography—Juvenile
literature. 4. Migrant agricultural laborers—Labor unions—United States—History—Juvenile literature.
5. United Farm Workers—History—Juvenile literature. I. Mattern, Joanne, 1963- author. II. Title.
HD6509.C48R665 2016
    331.88'13092—dc23 [B]   2015027871

Produced by Spooky Cheetah Press
Poem by Jodie Shepherd
Design by Keith Plechaty

© 2016 by Scholastic Inc.

All rights reserved. Published in 2016 by Children's Press, an imprint of Scholastic Inc.

Printed in China 62

SCHOLASTIC, CHILDREN'S PRESS, ROOKIE BIOGRAPHIES®, and associated logos are trademarks
and/or registered trademarks of Scholastic Inc.

1 2 3 4 5 6 7 8 9 10 R 25 24 23 22 21 20 19 18 17 16

Photographs: cover: George Ballis/The Image Works; 3 top left: Cathy Murphy/Getty Images; 3 top
right: KRT/Newscom; 3 bottom: Madlen/Shutterstock, Inc.; 4: Cathy Murphy/Getty Images; 8: Horace
Bristol/Corbis Images; 11: Walter P. Reuther Library, Wayne State University; 12: Science and Society/
Superstock, Inc.; 15: Cathy Murphy/Getty Images; 16: Michael Rougier/The LIFE Picture Collection/
Getty Images; 19, 20, 23: 1976 George Ballis/The Image Works; 24: Jason Laure/The Image Works;
27: Bettmann/Corbis Images; 28: Arthur Schatz/The LIFE Picture Collection/Getty Images; 29
left: George Ballis/The Image Works; 29 right: Cathy Murphy/Getty Images; 31 top: Science and
Society/Superstock, Inc.; 31 center top: Jason Laure/The Image Works; 31 center bottom: George
Ballis/The Image Works; 31 bottom: FPG/Getty Images.

Map by Terra Carta

Table of Contents

Meet Cesar Chavez

Cesar Chavez grew up very poor. His family traveled from place to place to find jobs. They worked very hard. During the day, they picked crops in the hot sun. At night, they often had to sleep on the side of the road.

As an adult, Chavez worked hard to improve the lives of all farmworkers.

Cesar (seh-SAHR) Chavez
(CHAH-vess) was born on
March 31, 1927, near Yuma, Arizona.
His family had their own farm.
The Chavez family was **Latino**.
They were originally from Mexico.

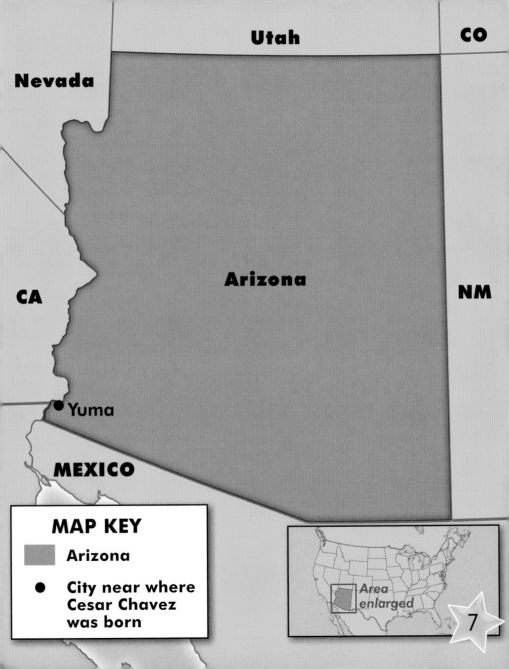

Utah

CO

Nevada

CA

Arizona

NM

● Yuma

MEXICO

MAP KEY

Arizona

● City near where
  Cesar Chavez
  was born

Area enlarged

7

Life changed for Cesar when he was about 10 years old. There was a very bad drought. No rain fell. Crops would not grow. Cesar's family could no longer afford to keep their farm. They became migrant workers. They traveled from town to town, looking for work picking crops.

Young Migrant Farmer

The Chavez family had to move all the time. Cesar went to more than 30 different schools before he was 13 years old. When he was not in school, he worked in the fields. His family never had enough money. When he was in eighth grade, Cesar quit school and went to work full-time.

This is a photo of Cesar in eighth grade.

Even though Cesar had to leave school, he kept on learning. He loved to read. He especially liked reading about people who changed the world. Cesar read about an **activist** named Mahatma Gandhi. Gandhi lived in India when it was ruled by Great Britain. He used peaceful ways to win freedom for his country.

Mahatma Gandhi

In 1943, Chavez met Helen Fabela. They fell in love. Three years later, Chavez joined the United States Navy. America was fighting in World War II. Chavez left the Navy in 1948. He and Helen got married. They would have eight children together.

Cesar and Helen in 1975

The Chavez family kept working on farms. Like other Latino migrant workers, they had very hard lives. There were no bathrooms in the field. The workers did not even have fresh water to drink! Chavez felt that migrant workers were not treated fairly by growers.

Migrant workers spent all day working in the hot sun.

Starting a Movement

Chavez wanted all the farmworkers to join together to change the way they were treated. In 1962, Chavez formed a **union**. It was called the National Farm Workers Association (NFWA). A union is a group of workers who join together to improve working conditions.

Chavez talks to farmworkers.

Huelga means "strike" in Spanish.

In 1965, Chavez heard about problems facing grape pickers in California. Their working conditions were terrible. Chavez and the NFWA led the workers in a strike. They refused to pick grapes. They said they would not work until they were given better pay and better working conditions.

FAST FACT!

In 1966, the NFWA became the United Farm Workers (UFW). Their motto was "*Sí, se puede.*" In Spanish this means "Yes, it is possible." That is like saying "Yes, we can."

The workers went to the fields during the day. They held up signs saying they were being treated unfairly. The growers tried to break up the demonstrations. They drove tractors through the fields. This sent up clouds of dust that choked the workers. Some workers were arrested. Others were beaten up! Through it all, the workers remained peaceful.

Growers try to chase
striking workers away.

Chavez speaks as supporters hold signs telling people to stop buying grapes.

A Nation United

The strike went on and on.
Then Chavez had a big idea.
He asked people all over America
to stop buying grapes from
California. This is called a **boycott**.
People listened. The growers lost
a lot of money.

Still, the strike continued. Chavez knew he needed another big idea. In February 1968, he began a fast. For 25 days, he did not eat anything. He drank only water. Finally, in 1970, the workers won! The growers made a new contract, or agreement, with the workers. Now they would receive better pay and health care. They would have better working conditions.

Chavez claps as a new
workers' contract is signed.

Timeline of Cesar Chavez's Life

1948
marries Helen Fabela

1927
born on March 31

1962
forms the National Farm Workers Association (NFWA) union

Chavez continued to fight for better conditions for farmworkers for the rest of his life. He died on April 23, 1993.

Cesar Chavez believed everyone should be treated fairly. Through his work, he made life better for millions of Latinos and other Americans.

1970
grape strike ends

1965
leads strike against grape growers

1993
dies on April 23

A Poem About Cesar Chavez

He saw conditions he did not like,
so Cesar Chavez led a strike.
He got the world to stop and care,
if migrant workers' lives were fair.

You Can Make a Difference

- Speak up if you see people being treated unfairly.

- Look for peaceful ways to solve problems.

- Work with others to solve problems in your school or community.

Glossary

activist (AK-tiv-ist): person who fights for social change

boycott (BOY-kot): refusal to buy a product to protest against the company that makes it

Latino (lah-TEE-no): someone from a Spanish-speaking country south of the United States

union (YOON-yuhn): group of people who work together to fight for fair conditions at their jobs

Index

Facts for Now

Visit this Scholastic Web site for more information on Cesar Chavez:
www.factsfornow.scholastic.com
Enter the keywords **Cesar Chavez**

About the Author

Anne Roome has taught in classrooms with second, seventh, and eleventh graders—and has loved every second of it.

Joanne Mattern has written more than 250 books for children. She especially likes writing biographies because she loves to learn about real people and the things they do.